AHHH LIFE

t. kilgore splake

25214 ash street
calumet, mi 49913
906-337-2917
splake@chartermi.net

TRANSCENDENT ZERO PRESS
HOUSTON, TEXAS

Copyright © 2017 t. kilgore splake.

PUBLISHED BY TRANSCENDENT ZERO PRESS
www.transcendentzeropress.org

All rights reserved. No part or parts of this book may be reproduced in any format, except for portions used in reviews, without the expressed written consent from the author or from the publisher.

ISBN-13: 978-1-946460-95-0

ISBN-10: 1-946460-95-8

Printed in the United States of America

Library of Congress Control Number: 2017946851

Cover design by Glynn Monroe Irby
Cover images: t. kilgore splake

FIRST EDITION
Transcendent Zero Press

AHHH LIFE

t. kilgore splake

25214 ash street
calumet, mi 49913
906-337-2917
splake@chartermi.net

raw prime
bloody beef patty
dark rye bread
large onion slice
garlic mustard
black pepper
christian brothers sip
waiting espresso
mad poet's breakfast
early morning feast

Thinking on the Unseen
Dustin Pickering

This collection from t. kilgore splake offers the reader something many of his other collections lack. splake, in his usual recollections, reveals the dark and light as well as those indifferent moments when he could have acted but didn't. Lust becomes an observer and failure or despondency is just a fact of life. These poems, the musings of an old bard set on attaining poetic heights, say something of the character of impressions more than anything.

splake's use of short, centered lines speaks volumes about his approach to poetics and memory. While his poems tend to reiterate common themes from his life, what makes for the magic is the nature of how those themes are communicated. Impressions are quick, indifferent, and yet we want to hold them and make them ours. splake's memories are anchored, and he releases them as a fisher would his prize fish.

Perhaps t. kilgore realizes the deeper nature of Fate when he writes, or contests with the Lady Muse. Poets engage in continuous agons with their words, memories, and the conflicted ideas that latch on to them. Never a dull moment in a thinker's mind. splake frequently unearths the shallowness of "gatekeepers" like MFA grads and flimsy poets. They are like the women who feign affection to receive gifts. splake pauses to let us breathe the ash of hypocrisy while he hides at his self-named Brautigan Creek.

Nothing is fake to the living observer except the emotionless popularity of those who pretend to play by the rules. Do what you are told to do by those you don't really respect so they will also pretend to respect you. Why do we seek this impersonal fame? We are vain creatures settling in the night, whispering in the dark: our song is only an answer if we are deep in solitude. splake, as the reader already knows, is aware of this.

Those familiar with his works already know his staccato recollections, his use of short "haiku-like" lines that form shapeless lyrics centered on the page. Does this mean anything specifically?

In my essay "On an Article's Absence: Poetic Style as Essential to Vision as Observed in Marcie Eanes' Poetry Works" I note that style is essential to what the author intends to convey through his or her writing. In the case of t. kilgore splake, his approach declares independence and testifies to life's centeredness within brief impressions. We are observers and actors in our lives. splake sees how much of life's harmony is sham, mere moments of touch-and-go or pretend friendship, but he also celebrates it as a deep resonance common to us all.

save the trees

simple easy answer
words not explaining
what's beneath the bark

# # # #

eternity

after artist's death
poems quickly forgotten
remote wilderness stream
he named brautigan creek
flowing on forever

# # # #

rolling road miles

felt it coming
pounding alpha-beat keys
couldn't type fast enough
30 feet today
another dozen tomorrow

# # # #

notyetnotyetnotyet

memory lapses
hemorrhoid ointment
metamucil in the mornings
after surgery prayer
they got it all

\# \# \# \#

cold turkey weekend

kicking thorazine fog
slowing brains thoughts
long night hours
sipping warm blue ribbons
lost in empty silence
waiting quiet whisper

# # # #

next victims

ignoring school education
classes and teachers
failures soon waiting
k-mart blue light
cheap ammunition
guns on sale

# # # #

beat goes on

mfa fugitives
ignored by major presses
chasing life's reality
beyond wine cheese parties
dreamers experimenting
challenging literary rules
not afraid to fail

# # # #

somebody's daughter

graybeard leech
older than her father
robbing family cradle
quest for perfect love
unconventional passions
beyond formula romance

# # # #

purple white cheers

lifetime chasing ghost
only one ever loved
young sexy cheerleader
refused movie date
not moving on
enjoying childish agony
instead of growing up

####

question of faith

dark night hours
steady lake superior waves
moving to rocky shore
softly whispering question
over and over again
anxious to answer
lacking words to reply

# # # #

escape

tranny tripping
dusty two-track roads
cold sixer on seat
almost insane poet
fighting severe depression
free from darkness
for a little while

# # # #

gray grizzled poet

clock ticking
playing extra innings
others dying of cancer
heart attacks and strokes
wondering if time
for rorschach painting
bloody brain art
staining bedroom wall

\# \# \# \#

enlightenment

abandoning lockstep life
society without variety
in world gone to shit
seeking meaning
like han shan
older chinese poets
living in mountains
lost in pale mist

# # # #

days of typer madness

chain smoking poet
lost in creative cloud
floating above
alpha beat keys
hypnotized by clacking letters
occasional pause
typewriter bell
signaling carriage return
before beginning again

# # # #

ideath

dust covered sketchbox
drawer for knives
section for paint tubes
warped empty canvas
lonely companion with
home workout gym
weekend garage sale specials
owners with failed dreams
never reaching other place

# # # #

journey into beginning

cold turkey weekend
lost in blurry hours
nights becoming mornings
hands shaking
choking dry heaves
screams caught in throat
praying to god
taste of cold one
forgetting wife and kids
letting brain escape

\# \# \# \#

literary madness

many cheap poets
never buying extra copy
journal with their poem
couple of dollars
helping small press freedom
or purchasing others' books
reading their ideas
discovering if telling lies
some creative artists
taking emotions deeper
describing pain better

# # # #

passing

october time of life
remembering forest brilliance
burning autumn colors
young innocent kiss
still burning lips
leaving aching heart
years quickly fading
dry warped leaves
telling graying poet
time to vanish
disappear in morning mist

# # # #

nuclear winter

dead arctic world

dusty winds blowing
across empty desert
clouds covering sun
daylight extinguished
leaving cold gray shadows
earth silent without
warm bird songs
because politicians failed
poets' words ignored

# # # #

untitled

greedy buying sprees
satisfying empty needs
forgetting beautiful things
soft white trillium
butterfly in flight
pine needle hum
brook trout rising
mayfly hatch
path's warm earth
surrounding poet's heart

# # # #

beyond disney

early morning
hungry yellow eyes
wilderness killing
just to stay alive
animals after prey
never giving up
sharp white teeth
celebrating forest feast
bloodstained remains
returning to the earth

# # # #

censor

sad lonely lady
art gallery volunteer
morally driven madness
losing paintings
trashing poetry books
serious creative works lost
like hadley
with hem's short stories
la gare station
mother's new baby
left at hospital

# # # #

lightness

shallow breaths
pale skin color
feverish sweating
end near
graying poet struggling
seeking right words
to finish final poem
explaining painful heart
inability to love
jigsaw puzzle with
pieces missing

# # # #

love gone south

beautiful young lady
can't say "i love you"
words impossible to imagine
sad relationship over
restless needy woman
greyhound ticket freedom
returning home to mother
black coffee mornings
camel straight nights
dark painful memories
little girl still missing
daddy not there

# # # #

keeping secrets

young lady dreamer
finding comfort in nature
her poems and photographs
capturing wilderness beauty
solitary artist
hungry for romance
desperate to be wanted
find true love
left to forest silence
lifetime channel movies
special afternoon soap
sad what ifs

# # # #

literary landscape

sad modern poets
ancient mfa degrees
talking instead of writing
holding author's conference
local yoga center
reading old poems
words from years ago
serious edgy voices
after presentations
dulcimer interlude
drinking spiced tea
chatting with visitors
new poems unwritten

# # # #

pilgrimage

escape society of things
leave shiny trinkets behind
abandon fences
no trespassing signs
enjoy powerful magic
peaceful cliffs retreat
learn wilderness wisdom
listening to earth
staring beyond clouds
impossible to get lost
take wrong paths
solitary odyssey
to where heart belongs

# # # #

throwback

typed original manuscript
over transom delivery
carbon copy in freezer
apartment fire insurance
starving artist
fearing rejection
hoping unknown reader
in slush pile pages
liking his voice
publishing company
inking rollers
firing up press
new novel title
brief taste of fame

# # # #

comes around

barbara quit writing
no more bitter poems
daughter growing up
terrors of family chaos
realizing other's work better
or tired of familiar
saying same old things
now understanding life
reading daily horoscopes
tarot cards and i-ching
seriously considering
pregnancy and childbirth
raising son or daughter
another single mother
repeating her mistakes

# # # #

second half of my life

long evening hours
steady lake superior tides
washing rocky shore
calm early darkness
before first morning light
leaking through clouds
today's world different
after yesterday's surprise
writing first poem
suddenly discovering
what life is about
devoting self to poetry
writing new creative works
ideas with meaning
after hot coffee

# # # #

the other side

rucksack wanderer
tarot card fool
fleece vest
redwing shitkicker boots
forest path vanishing
in maze of dark shadows
lightning flashes close
loud thunder explosions
wind stinging face
storm rapidly moving
suddenly feeling invisible
beyond sound and fury
hearing whisper
not god mother or wife
but my voice saying
poet be free

# # # #

next poem

soon life's memories
feel like distant dreams
disappearing into clouds
blurry snowglobe blizzard
marrying twice
fathering sons and daughter
college professor
teaching twenty-four years
serious graybeard romance
attractive young girl
intelligent poet
raising young daughter
steely determination
make it work this time
now today's reality
sound of scratching pen
filling empty page

# # # #

poetic rapture

eighty year old graybeard
still only sixteen
early morning's face
bathroom mirror reflection
flirting with young barista
cooking café espresso
sharing her new poem
recent camera photos
unlike mfa poets
both of us certain
feelings are everything
barbara comfortable with
easter birthdays christmas
grandmothers and flowers
having 'nice days'
without intense passions
cocks tits cunts

# # # #

becoming

alphabet blocks
tinkertoys and erector set
balsa-tissue model planes
not into books
reading others stories
or hopelessly lost
in encyclopedia pages
enjoying outdoors
playing ball games
hiking remote wilderness
seeking magic places
like larva in cocoon
enzymes chemically mixing
emerging new being
suddenly a poet
choosing different words
creating new dreams

# # # #

going home

(moment of faith)

hoping to achieve grace
like agnes facing death
ingmar bergman film
"cries and whispers"
denying suicide escape
like papa hem and brautigan
cremation and estate
for attorney and others
soon pain gone
angry cruel behaviors
warm gentle kindness
lost in forgotten time
wondering if angels
helping with journey
if heaven has music
different from rock 'n roll

# # # #

roman holiday

married audrey three times
after insane romances
candle light dinners
dancing until morning
sleeping on artist's sofa
soon rocking chair miles
early morning colic
reading doctor seuss
learning abcs
before abandoning family
leaving home sweet home
joining friend of the court
child support dues
now should understand
dangers of young love
yet telling new princess
"merry christmas" darling
holiday gifts wrapped
under the tree

# # # #

learning to read

elementary school class
sitting in different circles
dick jane spot
capital letters and periods
teacher's paper page guide
so not looking ahead
getting confused
or finishing story early
teaching conventional behavior
suppressing creativity
not nurturing rebels
educating boys
who rigidly salute
reply "yes sir"
girls going to college
learning *ibids* and *op cits*
new primer authors
with wooden characters
story still saying nothing

####

mad memories

old route 66
mother road mainstreet
concrete avenue to nirvana
for steinbeck's oakies
road for kerouac
looking for himself
café waitress
"good mornin' hon"
imaginary romantic dreams
speedometer miles turning
new surprise waiting
around next highway bend
unknown artist creating
large blue whale
car radio whispers
bobby troupe's ballad
chicago to l.a.
don't forget winona
old san berdoo

# # # #

hollywood dreams

purple-white shouts
loudly cheering wildcats
three rivers athletic heroes
friday night sockhop
high school gym
after game finished
finding new loves
during long slow dances
exchanging class rings
lasting week or two
following breakup
finding another friend
negotiating with dad
car and date money
convincing mother
new prom dress necessary
teenagers not actors
but deserve oscar fame

####

forgotten works

brief moment
passing at brautigan creek
piney woods path
beyond cobblestone chimney
american mine ruins
below granite cliffs
watery musical melodies
gentle reminder
of richard's fine poetry
catfish friends
candlelions
perfect days
marcia a-plus
also remembering
rocking chair miles
nights long ago
songs for baby daughter
soft soothing words
taking anxious casey
back to sweet dreams

# # # #

gray 'beat' ghost

living in old paperbacks
used e-bay titles
amazon one-cent specials
regularly contesting
elusive dame lady muse
wrestling rat bastard time
daily naps important
deep death respites
tarot card fool
on solitary pilgrimage
eternally questing
while other people
lost in plato's cave
worshipping flag
accepting political economics
leaving poor starving
abandoning their children
believing in god
blindly ignoring
wars and natural disasters
opaque sea of faces
prisoners of illusions

\# \# \# \#

beyond the cliffs

climbing together
until trail suddenly narrowed
morning birdsong silent
only sounds of our breaths
young lady hiker
enjoying new adventure
with graybeard companion
old man's slow steps
like aging pilgrim
el camino santiago trek
renewing spiritual energy
listening for ghosts
voices from forgotten past
digging in ruins
seeking native arrowheads
pipes buttons combs
from miners' home sites
reading cemetery headstones
history of lives past
realizing world still continues
finally reaching summit
enjoying quiet rest

momentarily lost
in each other's heart

# # # #

pretender

sad lost poet
kindergarten to mfa
artificial suburban roots
easy campus life
suddenly facing problems
broken-hearted romance
death coming near
pretending nature has answers
occasional walk in woods
doesn't make connection
becoming one with wilderness
like god
dark night hours
understanding owls call
soaring on hawks wings'
riding warm thermals
with millions of butterflies
flitting here and there
living inside nighttime storm
loud crashing thunder
lightning streaking across sky

finally feeling peace
winds calming
evening noise fading
forest silent again

\# \# \# \#

seeing clearly

johnny nash lyrics
ricocheting around my skull
graybeard poet in survival mode
following romantic breakup
hopelessly in love
with beautiful young lady
feeling sixteen years old again
woman faking affection
playing on my emotions
selfishly accepting gifts
buying word processor
new school clothes
regular monthly check
starving artist funds
sad child
unable to love
made serious commitment
waiting to grow up
still no regrets
over foolish lust

caring what others think
real life beginning
writing new poems
publishing small book
bunny boiling ex-mate
waiting for someone else

\# \# \# \#

coming of age

weary graying man
rare moment musing
never seeing country
long motorcycle trip
touring blue highways
living in old van
swimming salty oceans
climbing real mountains
standing on summit
wondering what's beyond
instead white collar lifer
wasting best years
earning steady dollars
monthly debts
mortgage and new car
credit card maxed
buying wife and kids
expensive gifts and toys
financing college education
masonic lodge membership
sword and feathered cap
mother becoming leader
eastern star and white shrine

imagine wild gossip
husband and father
declaring himself a poet
"carpe diem" moment
chasing artistic dream
free as the wind

# # # #

new beginning

hearing soft whispers
following papa's voice
back to sucker river
north of seney
village train station
blazing new path
beyond two-tire roads
old logging trails
using forest switchbacks
avoiding flooded marshes
remember danger waiting
for solitary hiker
traveling light
instant coffee
old stained pot
pouch of pipe tobacco
hudson bay blanket
finding beaver pond
hem's camp site
place he abandoned demons
healing ww-i wounds
later his words created
"big two-hearted river"

achieving literary fame
tired college professor
lost empty feelings
troubles with coping
simply getting by
hoping hemingway odyssey
creative new direction
finally discovering
who i shall become
# # # #

wannabe poets

university professors
mfa celebrities
safe academic tenure
nervous posturings
over grant-in-aid dollars
coffeeshop blowhards
loud mouth talkers
like joe gould
telling frequent lies
composition books filled
with same familiar lines
others like grimm's dwarves
doc dopey happy
shy smiling faces
mixing up their words
laughing at themselves
people without soul
deep emotional feelings
visions focused on
life and death
changing of the seasons

or rebel poets
flirting with madness
living on edge
describing society's chaos
insanity below the rim
killing demons
like dylan thomas
full of irish whiskey
virginia woolf
counting stones
to fill her pockets
wading in river currents
swimming away forever

\# \# \# \#

mister 'nice guy'

young attractive barista
boiling morning espresso
long fleshy legs
connecting leather sandals
with faded denim cutoffs
soft sexy breasts
snug in lycra t
sad young girl
recently playing with dolls
having happy daydreams
suddenly scared of poverty
prisoner of steady job
needing to save dollars
insure future security
without chasing passions
working with the arts
thinking of normal husband
happy marriage
avoiding life's useless dramas
man shining shoes
wearing suit and tie

no shabby clothes
unlaced kicker boots
buying nice things
new car
not backlot special
fancy furniture
no lumpy sofa
partner for sunday services
weekly spiritual purification
not demanding silence
for solitary poet
pushing driven imagination
seeking new words
regularly writing poems
describing something better

# # # #

olga's gone

like paul
brando movie character
"last tango in paris"
married woman with money
new wife olga
ex-pat swiss citizen
living in united states
older sophisticated lady
not worrying over
my serious drinking
maybe helping me
get my kids back
living with their father
surprised sudden shock
shaking nervous system
drunken morning
discovering her body
bloody bathtub waters
wrist arteries slashed
wondering what to do
call police department
local hospital emergency

cold naked remains
wrapped in body bag
following ambulance
flashing lights off
small quiet funeral
card and flower sympathies
sober conversation
talking with her son
later family attorney
question of inheritance
details of surviving estate
dark future moments
lonely poet wondering
about wife's sudden violence
why she killed herself

# # # #

t. kilgore splake

t. kilgore splake ("the cliffs dancer") lives in a tamarack location old mining row house in the ghost copper mining village of calamut in michigan's upper peninsula. as an artist, splake has become a legend in the small press literary circles for his writing and photography. his most recent book is "ghost light" published by "gage press" in battle creek, michigan. also, slake has several black and white photographs in the new issue of "clutch" published by street corner press in sister bay, wisconsin. splake is currently collecting historical materials for a chapbook on the old railroad depot in calamut, michigan.

www.ingramcontent.com/pod-product-compliance
Lightning Source LLC
Chambersburg PA
CBHW031502040426
42444CB00007B/1173